OLD GARDEN ROSES

OLD GARDEN ROSES

AND SELECTED MODERN HYBRIDS

Photographs by *Josh Westrich*

Texts by *Eva Dierauff and Anny Jacob*

Foreword by *Helene von Stein-Zeppelin*

With 166 illustrations, 83 in color

THAMES AND HUDSON

Note on terminology

In 1971 the World Federation of Rose Societies accepted
a new system of classifying roses. However, the older,
traditional names are still widely used and have
accordingly been adopted in this book. The main
examples are the following: 'perpetual' now classified as
'recurrent'; 'Floribunda' now classified as 'Cluster-
flowered bush'; 'hybrid tea' now classified as 'Large-
flowered bush'.

I am particularly grateful to Richard Huber, Anny
Jacob, Heide Nolte, Gerald Singel and Helene von
Stein-Zeppelin for their energetic support.

Translated from the German *Die Rose: alt und erlesen* by
Keith Thomas

First published in the United States in 1988 by
Thames and Hudson Inc., 500 Fifth Avenue,
New York, New York 10110

Library of Congress Catalog Card Number 88-50228

Printed and bound in Hong Kong

CONTENTS

Foreword

THE HISTORY OF THE ROSE stretches far back into time, and we can only guess how long mankind has appreciated this flower. But it is for the rose lover of today that this book – the photographs and the texts – was produced. The rose portraits, some of them almost ethereal in their effect, will appeal equally to the enthusiastic gardener, both professional and amateur, and to all those lovers of plants whose eyes and senses are receptive to the pure beauty, the wonderful variety of form, the immense richness of colour, and the fragile delicacy of the rose. Josh Westrich has studied his idiosyncratic models with the sympathetic eyes of a true artist, and made use of his considerable talent to emphasize the true character of each rose. He shows the red roses in their full, luminous glory, captures every nuance of the lighter-toned blooms, and brings out to the full the capricious nature of the white varieties. Entrancing details set each scene. This collection of pictures forms a unique, charming and seductive rose roundelay.

The aesthetic appeal of the rose is by no means its only fascination; our cultural inheritance is inextricably intertwined with it. The history of the rose's triumphal march around the globe is rich and exciting. Fables, legends and myths have woven a thick garland around this queen of flowers. Since time immemorial innumerable poets and philosophers have dedicated their verse and their prose to the rose. Composers have spun countless melodies around it. Painters and sculptors have created timeless works of art with the rose as subject. The Christian church long ago raised the rose from its earth-bound roots, and dedicated it to the mother of God. The worlds of medicine, cooking and cosmetics have all prized rose essences. Above all, however, the rose has remained the symbol of love and worship for thousands of years.

In this book the roses are allowed to speak their own glorious, pictorial language. They reveal to us every stage in the gradual process of flowering and decay, from the first, tiny green bud to the fully opened bloom. Every shade of the rose, from the spotless milk white, through soft yellow and all the variations of pink, to deep wine red and mauve, is to be found on these pages. The brilliant light of day lends these roses a shimmering transparency. This volume takes us into an imaginary rose garden, dominated by the glorious 'old' varieties with their delicious scents, but embracing many wild roses, charming and appealing in their simplicity. Of the hundreds of varieties cultivated in our century, Josh Westrich found only a few which embodied the harmonious qualities required to round off this flourishing ensemble. The pictures are simply astounding, worthy of anybody's eyes and time; they awake memories and one day, perhaps, will become reality in our own gardens.

Helene von Stein-Zeppelin

HELENE VON STEIN-ZEPPELIN
Laufen, November 1987

The rose in history and culture

Eva Dierauff

THE ROSE — even its name is pleasing to the ear — conjures up images of little wild dog roses, cheerful in their simplicity; of garden parties set amid pastel colours or deep, saturated hues; of the unique, velvet softness and symmetry of individual blooms. Roses are sheer poetry: growing, budding, flowering poetry. For countless ages they have moved the heart and mind of man. In their beauty — sometimes soft, sometimes powerful — and their seductive fragrance they are the very embodiment of summer. At first the green mantle allows the tiny coloured points to peep forth timidly. The day's light and warmth give the calyx the strength and courage to spread into the awakening morning. Full of misgivings, the pure, virginal bud puffs itself out, until the fire of the midday sun forces it to burst open. Its foliage is distinctive, its countenance beautiful, yet full of character. With incomparable grace the rose lives out its short span, to the delight of those who look at it and to the ecstasy of the bees which swarm giddily around it.

It was thousands of years ago that mankind first succumbed to the magic and variety of the rose. These men may well have lived in Asia, the original home of the rose. A clay tablet dating from 1200 BC, found in the Palace of Nestor in Crete, speaks of rose-scented oil. Writing in the third century before Christ, Theophrastus, the father of botany, reported that the inhabitants of Philippi brought wild roses to their gardens from the mountain of Pangaeus, where they were prospecting for gold. Charlemagne commanded that roses should be grown in monastery gardens, albeit for medicinal use rather than for decoration. The herbals of the Middle Ages paint a picture of the roses cultivated in Germany at that time: these were white, pink and red species, with few petals. The first yellow roses did not reach Europe until around 1600, when Carolus Clusius, the famous botanist and doctor, brought home the first examples from the Ottoman Empire. *Hortus Eystettensis*, which the apothecary Basilius Besler published around the same time, contains a wealth of fine plant illustrations, and among them we can recognize *Rosa gallica*, *Rosa × alba*, *Rosa damascena* and *Rosa × centifolia*, which remained the most important of the European garden roses until the second half of the eighteenth century. The perpetual Portland, Noisette, Bourbon and remontant roses were not developed until after the introduction of *Rosa × chinensis*, originating in China, and of the tea roses, *Rosa × odorata*.

The rose in history

The rose theme reaches far back into history. As Walter de la Mare said: 'Oh, no man knows/Through what wild centuries/Roves back the rose' ('All That's Past'). As ever, the Greeks sought the answer to the inexplicable amongst the gods. When Aphrodite rose out of the sea, the mother-of-pearl foam which clung to her was transformed into white roses, and nectar from heaven imparted the everlasting scent to them. En route to her wounded lover Adonis, the beautiful Aphrodite scratched herself on a thorn, whereupon her blood coloured the rose petals red. Sappho, the lyric poet of the island of Lesbos which had cultural links with the goddess, wrote an ode to the rose, honouring it with the title 'Queen of Flowers'. According to Indian mythology, Lakshmi, the keeper of fortune and wealth, slumbered in a rose bud made of 108 large, and 1008 small, rose petals. The Mohammedans believe that the founder of their religion, like Christ, ascended into heaven, and shed a drop of perspiration during his ascent to higher spheres. The drop fell on earth, and from it sprang the white rose. The prophet's companion, the Archangel Gabriel, also lost one drop of sweat, and the red rose grew from the place where it had fallen. The prophet's donkey was transported with them, and the single drop of sweat from the beast produced the yellow rose. Out of the commonplace comes the extraordinary, and the red and yellow rose were born. The Al-Khalid brothers of Iraq wrote in verse of the two-coloured, red and yellow rose which flowered in their country in the tenth century. In the nineteenth century Friedrich Rückert translated the verses into German. It is clear that the history of the rose cannot be separated from the history of man. Just as silk found its way to Europe from the Far Eastern empires via the old trade routes through central Asia – the silk road – the rose may also have migrated westward in the course of the millennia. An astonishing fact is that the Damask rose is still widely known as the 'Rose of Castile' in America.

Around the same time disputes blazed up in Great Britain between the Houses of York and Lancaster, concerning the right of succession to the throne. The battle symbol of the former was the white rose, and of the latter the red rose. In his play *Henry VI* Shakespeare set the scene of the quarrel between the 'kingmakers' and their opponents in the rose garden of the Temple of London: 'Since you are tongue-tied and so loath to speak,/In dumb significants proclaim your thoughts./Let him that is a true-born gentleman/And stands upon the honour of his birth,/If he suppose that I have pleaded truth,/From off this brier pluck a white rose with me' (Plantagenet). 'Let him that is no coward nor no flatterer,/But dare maintain the party of the truth,/Pluck a red rose from off this thorn with me' (Somerset). For thirty years the 'Wars of the Roses' raged, until the bloody fight was settled by the political marriage of King Henry VII, a Tudor, to Princess Elizabeth of York. 'We shall unite the white and the red rose. May Heaven smile upon this just union.' From this time on, the red Tudor rose with its white centre had a unique place in English heraldry.

Several centuries later the rose was adopted as heraldic symbol on the coats of arms of some American states including Georgia, New York, Iowa and North Dakota. A report concerning the Seven Years' War, dating from 1759, claims that roses can spur men on to feats of heroism in the turmoil of battle. The English fusiliers, ordered to Minden to support the Prussian regiments, took up quarters in a rose garden prior to the battle. With the courage born of desperation, they stuck roses in their helmets, ignored the danger, and won a famous victory. The 'rose-noble', a coin introduced by Edward IV in 1465, was said to be an effective good-luck charm for mariners. The coin, which shows a ship on the obverse and an eight-petalled rose on the reverse, became a symbol of British naval power. In her vanity, Queen Elizabeth I ordered that all coins of the realm were to be stamped with her rose-bordered portrait. However, this was by no means the first use of the rose in numismatics. In 400 BC the tetradrachm of Rhodes — the rose island — bore a beautiful rose. In a later period Italy produced the 'pistole della rosa' and the 'livornini della rosa'. In Germany the 'Rosenpfennig' ('rose penny') was in circulation.

The rose in the great gardens

Our image of the Versailles epoch is a mixture of the romantic and the gallant. The Marquise de Pompadour, mistress of Louis XV, was fully aware of the seductive qualities of roses, and their ability to enhance her feminine allure. Seldom did she make a public appearance without a rose bouquet at her bosom, or a garland lining the hem of her robe. Her successor in the favour of the monarch, Madame du Barry, slept under a lavish rose canopy, 'whose long, sweeping silk curtains were embroidered with patterns of cascading roses'. Her fate was anything but rosy – her life was cut short by the guillotine. Another obsessive rose enthusiast whose life was as dramatic as it was brief, was Josephine de Beauharnais, wife of Napoleon and Empress of France; unfortunately she was childless, and was subsequently repudiated. In establishing the sensational gardens at Malmaison, Josephine built for herself a rose memorial. Enjoying the pecuniary security of an empress, Josephine was able to spend a fortune in the pursuit of her passion for plants. She sent ships to every part of the globe to bring rare and exotic plants back to Malmaison. During the war between England and France the British admiralty granted her vessels special leave to pass the English naval blockade. Of all plants, roses were her particular interest. Over two hundred varieties were cultivated by her Scottish head gardener Hewartson.

Her boundless enthusiasm undoubtedly provided a stimulus to gardeners and rose lovers within France and without, but Josephine's reputation would surely have faded like the glory of the Napoleonic empire had she not suggested to Pierre-Joseph Redouté that he paint the roses. We can thank his precise brushwork for showing later generations details of many of the varieties grown at Malmaison. The first edition of Redouté's work *Les Roses*, with text by Thory, appeared between 1817 and 1824. However, it would be a disservice to Redouté to consider his accurate rose representations as no more than a botanical reference book. Nobody can come face to face with one of his original rose watercolours and fail to be deeply moved. 'But who can deny his homage to the rose, the queen of flowers that spring chose for its garland, that love picked for its bouquet. Yet only in our gardens do you thrive, you daughters of the dew and the morning star' (Voigt).

Thanks to their pure beauty, immense variety and strong scent, roses now bloom in almost every garden, rambling over pergolas, fences and verandas, filling flower beds, lining paths and attracting lovers of beauty of all ages to the wonderful rose gardens of our globe. One of the most attractive is 'La Bagatelle' in the Bois de Boulogne. In 1777 the Comte d'Artois, brother of Louis XVI, wagered Marie Antoinette that he could build a small palace within the space of three months. The reason for the great urgency was a festival planned to celebrate the return of the court to Versailles. With the help of 900 men the Comte completed the project in 64 days, won the bet, and relieved the Austrian-born lady of 100,000 livres. Periodically the estranged Josephine would creep off to Bagatelle to watch Napoleon's son playing – not her offspring, but Marie-Louise's. Around 1900 a rose garden worthy of the history of the site was laid out, where today 7,000 roses unfold their delicate blooms.

The rose garden of l'Haÿ near Paris, which includes a small open-air theatre, is a living rose museum. In June it is a capricious dream of a garden; filled with French *esprit*, and featuring a *temple de l'amour* which is covered with roses. A yet more exotic display is provided by the climbing roses in the Rosaleda in Madrid. 'Invariably we experience our most intense pleasure in the garden when all ecstasy of form suddenly appears as if suspended, and after the long, austere period of budding the simple, blessed form of the rose rises up before us' (the German poet Carossa). In 1827 the court gardener Schmidtmann must have felt somewhat less than joyful when he 'was placed under court arrest, put behind bars, and detained at His Majesty's pleasure', because he had concealed 300 rose standards. When the Kurfürst resolved to rejuvenate the park at Wilhelmshöhe near Kassel, he ordered a total of 10,000 rose plants to be brought from all the court gardens. In an earlier period Graf Friedrich II, the grandfather of Wilhelm II, had established the first German rose garden in the same park, then known as Weissenstein Park, where his head gardener was Herr Schwarzkopf. During the Napoleonic era a very large number of roses migrated from here to Malmaison – but the traffic was not entirely one way.

The rose in legend and fairy tale

'Neither the world, nor the imagination, can comprehend the rose' (the Persian poet Rumi). Countless tales and fables have been woven around roses. On the rear wall of Hildesheim Cathedral there is a 30-foot high, 40-foot wide rose. It is said that the plant, known as the 'thousand year rose', was actually planted by Charlemagne or Louis the Pious as thanks for divine protection from the threat of wild animals, but nobody can say for sure. The Persian poet Sadi tells of his encounter with a rose: 'hemmed in by tall grasses and stalks. "What?" I cried, "Are these common plants so impudent that they crowd round the splendid rose?" In a moment I was tearing out the grass, when suddenly a thin stalk bowed low to me, and said: "Don't do it! Spare me! I love her! I know that I am not worthy of the rose, but from the fine scent you can at least tell that I stand by her side".' Sadi showed mercy, because 'the rose enriches and beautifies the most pitiful and wretched, even the insubstantial grass.'

The centrepoint of the mid-thirteenth-century French epic poem 'Le Roman de la Rose' is a rose bud. In a dream the hero arrives at the garden of desire. The allegorical figure of idleness invites him to enter. The image of a rose is reflected in the spring of Narcissus. An ardent love blazes up in the young man. 'Alarmed and heavy of heart I felt more pain than wonder. And yet some inner force led me to the rose, which I found so beautiful.' The other characters, some good, some evil, try to help or hinder his suit. In the end he becomes the slave of the love god, who wants to help him. Yet when almost within reach of the object of his desire, he is bitterly forced to acknowledge that envy has built an impenetrable rampart around the one he worships.

In the twelfth century the Persian poet Nizami wrote his book *Treasury of Mysteries*. In it he writes of two rival physicians who attempted to poison each other. One of them swallowed the deadly pill, but was able to take the antidote in time. The second physician cast a spell on a rose, and when his rival sniffed it, he collapsed in his death throes. It was not the magic spell which killed him, but his knowledge of it. 'Snow White and Rose Red' by the Brothers Grimm is by no means so gloomy. The virtuous and unsuspecting maidens allow the bear into their warm room and stroke his fur. In the spring he leaves, and only reappears to free the two honest girls from an ugly dwarf. The spell is broken – the bear turns into a handsome prince. After another prince had woken his 'little thorn rose' the story might well have been repeated, as an old German epic poem confides: for thirty hours on end he kissed her laughing, rose-tinted lips.

Oscar Wilde's prose story 'The Nightingale and the Rose' is both sad and moving. A love-sick student looks in vain for a red rose, as his beloved refuses to dance with him until he brings her one. The nightingale hears his lament. 'Like a shadow she sailed through the grove', begging every rose bush for a red rose. But some were white, others yellow. Finally she found one stiffened by frost. 'If you want a red rose,' said the tree, 'you must build it out of music by moonlight, and stain it with your own heart's blood. You must sing to me with your breast against a thorn. All night long you must sing to me, and the thorn must pierce your heart, and your life-blood must flow into my veins, and become mine.' The little nightingale did not baulk at the high price demanded. 'Bitter, bitter was the pain, and wilder, wilder grew her song, for she sang of the love that is perfected by death . . . And the marvellous rose became crimson like the rose of the Eastern sky.' Yet the sacrifice was for nothing. The maiden disdained the rose. 'What a silly thing love is,' said the student as he walked away.

In the fable 'La Belle et le Monstre' ('Beauty and the Beast'), a merchant's daughter has a burning desire for a rose, and begs her father to bring one home from his travels. On his way home he finds an apparently deserted castle, and cuts a bud from a bush in its garden. The owner, a ghastly monster, threatens to kill the thief, unless he promises to give him his daughter in marriage. Beauty agrees, in order to save her father. She goes to the Beast, and at first feels sympathy for him. Gradually she begins to love him. Her courage is rewarded – the cursed prince is released from the spell. And they lived happily ever after.

The rose in poetry

From ancient times to the present, authors have written poems linking yearning and love with the rose. 'The rose bud, moist from the morning dew, laughs like the mouth of the beautiful Shirin. A thousand half-unfolded roses blush at the whisperings and caresses of half-concealed lovers.' With these happy words Mizra Kasim described the first awakening. A Malay poem expresses the idea of the rose, born to give pleasure: 'Amidst the rows of aromatic flowers thou, Rose, art the most splendid. The rose blossoms as a sun amongst stars.' In his fifty-fourth sonnet Shakespeare takes it one step further. 'O, how much more doth beauty beauteous seem/By that sweet ornament which truth doth give!/ The rose looks fair, but fairer we it deem/For that sweet odour which doth in it live.' Poetry to the magical unfolding of a flower at the tip of a delicate stem. Exactly why roses became the focus of so much admiration, why poets strove to weave their finest verses around them, why they became the universal symbol of love, is difficult to say. Perhaps Angelus Silesius provided the most fitting answer to the question: 'Ask not why of the rose; she flowers because she flowers. She takes no heed, she does not ask to be seen.' If a man looks at a rose, his sorrows vanish. 'Roses strewn on the path and grief is forgotten!' (Hölty). Or: 'Take the rose as your model! Sun, dew and the sweet wind from the East, she knows how to take freely and without anxiety all the brilliance and all the happiness of the earth . . .' (Hafiz). Parallel lines of thought in these German and Persian writers link the rose and love.

Writing around 1200, the German poet Walther von der Vogelweide took delight in the beauty of women, and wrote these casual words: 'If I could only pick roses with my dearest; so dearly would I caress her, that we would remain friends for ever.' A verse from the Middle Ages runs: 'Maiden, may I go with thee to thy rose garden? I would lead thee, sweet love, to the place where the red roses grow.' Klopstock expressed his feelings in less chivalrous terms, but perhaps more philosophically: 'In the shadows of spring I found her, and there I wrapped rose garlands round about her.' Goethe, on the other hand, has only one modest demand: 'There she stands, surrounded by roses, as young as any rose. One glance, beloved life! And that is reward enough.'

Roses – what an unfathomable source of inspiration! Melancholy and presentiments of death cling to the fading, withering flower petals, which already have a transitory air about them. 'The rise and decline of the rose's spirit – from life's creation to its decline.' Rilke's thought-provoking lines echo the paradox: 'Rose, o pure contradiction of desire; to be nobody's sleep amongst so many eyelids.' The poet raises the rose to a transcendental level, into the world of mysticism, as companion of fervent love and of cold death. Gottfried Keller tentatively sought to bridge those great gulfs, from which there is no return: 'The rose, the rose, so sweetly scented; the morning praises her to the skies! She flowers, and the ageing gardener earns his wages, but his eyes are full of sorrow and foreboding. He who enjoyed his own spring yesterday, sees the flower withered today – yet if a rose could think, no gardener would ever die.' The tragically transitory nature of life, the terrible sadness of experiencing inescapable fate alone, is echoed in Thomas Moore's melancholy words: ''Tis the last rose of summer,/Left blooming alone;/All her loving companions/Are faded and gone;/No flower of her kindred,/No rose-bud is nigh,/To reflect back her blushes,/Or give sigh for sigh.' And the Austrian poet Nikolaus Lenau, on seeing a withered rose, was plagued by the question:

'O heart of man, what is thy fortune? One moment, born in mystery, scarcely noticed, lost, never to be repeated?' In simpler, but no less heartfelt words, the German poet Mörike wrote of man's inconstancy, which manifests itself in faithlessness: 'Rose time! How swiftly, swiftly you are gone! If my love could only stay faithful, faithful, I would have nothing to fear.' Goethe's lines from the 'Heideröschen' ('Little heath rose') are equally simple, but profound: 'The little rose said, "I shall prick you, so that you will think of me always, yet I will not feel it".' Wilhelm Busch approached the subject of roses in a humorous vein: 'The rose spoke to the maiden: "I am eternally grateful to you, for pressing me to your bosom and bestowing your grace on me." The maiden spoke: "O little rose mine, do not imagine that you delight my eye and heart. I love you because you make me look pretty".' Roses possess unusual powers of flowering and propagating, but the words of the poets have surely enhanced their reputation.

The rose in cosmetics, cooking and medicine

'The spirit will find new wings if it refreshes itself with the sweet scent of roses.' So speaks the Persian poet Rumi. Ever since men learned to enjoy the pleasant fragrance of flowers, they have tried to preserve the rose's scent. The ancient Egyptians, Greeks and Romans perfected a process for adding the scent of rose petals to vegetable oil, and the method which the Indian Princess Nur Mahal used to obtain 'Attar' has survived to this day. She ordered rose petals to be thrown into a large basin of water. The sun's heat would cause a fine film of rose oil to form on the water's surface. The oil would be absorbed into soft cotton, which was then sealed in bottles. This seductive substance – still the essential ingredient of all great perfumes today – reached the zenith of its popularity in eighteenth-century France. To meet the demand roses were intensively cultivated, principally *Rosa gallica*, *Rosa damascena*, *Rosa × alba* and

Rosa × centifolia. These varieties had the reputation of giving off a scent which was erotically stimulating. Using modern production methods, 11,000 lb. of rose petals are required to produce 2 lb. of rose oil. In the nineteenth century, when the technology was more primitive, the yield must have been many times smaller.

Amongst the now-forgotten customs of the time was the practice of setting out pot-pourri bowls. These were shallow containers filled with rose petals soaked in alcohol, whose fresh aroma spread around the house for weeks. Another way of giving one's nose pleasure was to make 'Parfum du Roi'. This concoction called for twelve spoonfuls of deep-red rose water, mixed with a spoonful of icing sugar. The mixture was then simmered slowly over hot coal embers. There was no shortage of invention in the kitchen. The book *Queen's Delight*, published in 1695, included a recipe for candied rose petals: 'Dip small rose petals in beaten egg white or a weak solution of gum arabic, and place them on a piece of parchment. Sprinkle sugar on both sides, and dry them in a warm place.' They were used as dainty sweetmeats, or to decorate tarts. The world of medicine was not slow to exploit the wonderful healing power of roses. A decoction of red roses was said to bring rapid relief from headaches and sore throats.

The rose and the church

Once upon a time a white rose and a lily flowered in Paradise. Adam asked his wife which of the two was the more beautiful. Eve could not decide. They called the Archangel Gabriel to settle the matter. He preferred the lily, because the rose pricked him when he tried to pick it. Evidently angels are as sensitive to thorns as we are. Much offended, the rose left the garden of Eden at the same time as Adam and Eve were driven out. And the moral of the story: 'The sweet scent of the rose is enough, there is no need to break the plant. And if you are content with the scent, then the thorn will not prick you' (Mirzwa). The heathens believed that the dog rose was the lover of the Germanic goddess Freya, and possessed her maternal powers of guardianship.

The Catholic church has bestowed on the rose the greatest possible honour since the early Middle Ages. Based on Isaiah's prophetic words, 'And there shall come forth a rod out of the stem of Jesse, and a Branch shall grow out of his roots', the Latin ecclesiastical text compares the Mother of God to a rose. The prophecy is also the basis for the fifteenth-century German Christmas carol: 'Es ist ein' Ros' entsprungen . . .' In the breviary of the holy rosary, Mary's words are recorded as follows: 'I have borne fruit like the rose.' The Lauretanian litany calls her 'thou mysterious rose', and the pilgrims' hymn 'Meerstern, ich dich grüsse' ('Star of the Sea, I greet thee') includes the words 'O rose without thorn, thou chosen of God, O Mary, save us'. In the original form of the rosary each 'Ave Maria' was represented by a carved rose, the beads commonly used today not supplanting them until much later. The rosary consists of fifteen decades, relating to the one hundred and fifty psalms. The number fifteen is based on the 'five mysteries of Mary'. 'This use of the number five is reminiscent of the fundamental number five pertaining to the Rosaceae, a genus of plants to which the roses belong: the rings of stamens number five, ten, fifteen . . .' The five-petalled rose also figures as the ornament on choir stalls and confessional seats, and is a symbolic reminder of the five wounds of Christ. 'The rose, which thine outer eye here sees, has flowered for eternity in God.' What a reverential utterance by Angelus Silesius! The five-pointed star of the rose flower has shone out both physically and metaphorically through the ages.

The rose, the symbol of purity in the Mother of God, has also featured in the glorious works of woodcarvers. In the *Annunciation* by Veit Stoss, which can be admired at St Lorenz in Nuremberg, the Madonna and the angel stand within a giant garland of symmetrical roses. Seven superimposed medallions illustrating scenes from the life of Mary complete a wonderful work of art. Tilman Riemenschneider's sensitive hands formed the *Madonna in a Garland of Roses* in the 'Maria im Weingarten' pilgrim church at Volkach. With unbelievable delicacy Stefan Lochner painted *The Virgin of the Rose Garden*. The Mother of God sits on the ground before the scented mass of flowers. A proud, innocent maiden standing before a golden backdrop, in the form of a curtain supported by little angels: a religious idyll.

More serious and severe, but filled with profound humility, Martin Schongauer's *Madonna of the Rose Bower* sits enthroned on the grass bank, her face turned away from the child, yet in silent communion with him. Red rose flowers peep out of the green foliage against a golden background. A miracle of colour is Mathias Grünewald's *Virgin and Child* from the Isenheim altar at Colmar. The infant, playing with the glittering beads of a rosary, smiles up to his mother as she caresses him. Nearby a rose bush is in flower. In Dürer's *Madonna of the Rose Garlands*, crowns of roses are presented by Mary to Emperor Maximilian and by Jesus to Pope Julius II. All around angels hand out rose garlands. Roses played a quite different role on the fourth Sunday of Lent, Rose Sunday, at St Peter's in Rome. On this day, according to custom, the Pope blessed a 'piece of jewelry decorated with precious stones'. This was the golden rose, also known as the 'rose of virtue', whose golden bud was filled with balm and musk. This piece of jewelry, known as the 'Rosa aurea', was sent by the Holy Father to the monarch of a Catholic state as a sign of friendship. The roses bestowed by the Pope were beautiful creations in the finest gold leaf, the flower often bearing a sapphire. A quotation from the message of greeting sent with the rose makes clear the Pope's purpose: 'Take this rose from our hand which, however unworthy, occupies the place of God on Earth, a rose . . . that most beautiful flower, which is the joy and crown of all the Saints . . .'

The rose in painting, art and music

The rose was a source of inspiration not only for poets but also for other artists. In the fourteenth century Taddeo Gaddi used the dog rose for his frescoes in the Spanish Chapel at Santa Croce in Florence. Red and white roses set in vases glow at the Virgin's feet in his *Virgin Enthroned* in the Uffizi. The biblical and the natural mingle harmoniously in Filippino Lippi's *Madonna in the Forest*, where the white rose intertwines with ferns and coltsfoot. Botticelli's painting *Primavera* is based on classical mythology. Amor hovers above Venus, apparently weightless in the air. The ground is strewn with flowers, and the goddess Flora wears a translucent robe of roses. In his ceiling fresco *Aurora*, the Bolognese master Guido Reni showed the goddess of dawn whirling roses in the air. Rubens' imagination was fired by roses as well as by voluptuous women. In his paintings sweet cherubs trail rose garlands around. In the seventeenth century the Dutch flower painters adopted the rose as a special motif. Ambrosius Bosschaert portrayed flowers hanging casually over the edge of a bowl, Jan Bruegel and Jan van Huysum painted vividly coloured rose bouquets in stylish vases.

In the eighteenth century we meet once more the proud rose enthusiasts Madame de Pompadour and Madame du Barry, depicted in the portraits by Boucher and Drouais surrounded by roses. In the *Progress of Love* by Fragonard a tender young maiden in the rose garden is surprised by a youth climbing over the wall. 'Painting flowers refreshes my brain,' said Renoir. His *Conversation with the Gardener*, in which the latter appears to be discoursing on a variety of rose, is airy, flooded in light, with a strong feeling of the open air. Claude Monet's *Women in the Garden* is full of freshness and life, with the contrasting interplay of sun and shadow. The woman with the red hair feels herself drawn to the white rose bush, while another woman, lost in thought, sniffs at a cluster of flowers. Klimt's *Roses under Trees* (1905–10) finally brings the history of the painted rose into the twentieth century.

Yet roses, as rich and many-faceted subjects for artists, did not appeal to painters alone. Since the time of Benvenuto Cellini (1500–71) roses have served as motifs for goldsmiths and jewellers. The genre reached its peak in the eighteenth century, when every master jeweller strove to produce the definitive diamond-studded masterpiece in the form of bunches and garlands of roses. Each tried to outdo the others in inventiveness and richness of ideas when representing this noble plant. 'Many pieces were fitted with concealed springs, so that the glittering flowers would nod and tremble at their wearer's least movement.'

Roses inspired all areas of art – even music. The Minnesingers flirted with them through the knights' castles, spiritual Marian hymns reverberated in cathedrals, nuns along the lower Rhine sang the following verse from the 'Rose song': 'Put the glass to your lips, in the roses! And drink it down to the bottom; there you will find the Holy Ghost at the appointed hour, in the roses.' The 'Heideröslein' became a popular traditional song, which was dashed off in a spirited style: 'Enjoy life while the lamp still glows, pick the rose, before it withers.' Handel set Heinrich Brockes's verse to music in the Baroque style: 'Flaming rose, adornment of the earth . . .' Orff's *Carmina Burana* includes the lines 'Welcome, thou light of the world, thou rose of the world, welcome.' In a less theatrical, but more artful style, Mozart's Figaro recommends to Cherubino: 'Now forget gentle entreaties, sweet caresses and the fluttering of rose to roses.' In *Der Rosenkavalier* by Richard Strauss, the embarrassed Sophie takes the silver rose, the symbol of love, from Oktavian's hand: 'She is like a rose from paradise. When have I ever been so happy?' In the Wilhelminian era the piano accompanied the 'Rose songs' of Prince Philipp zu Eulenburg. The rose was even used as the centrepiece of a ballet. Nijinski's breathtaking leaps received spectacular acclaim in *Le Spectre de la Rose*. As the spirit of the rose he danced around the dreaming maiden, weaving his spell, and brought back to her the happiness of the previous night's ball. In the subterranean empire of the Venusberg, Tannhäuser comes upon red roses, and in *Parsifal* the maidens dress themselves in flowers. Whether music or speech – roses kindle powerful feelings, set atmospheric moods. They are not whimsical, they are simply beautiful. Let us end with Heinrich Heine's simple words: '. . . if you see a rose, tell her I send my regards.'

Opposite:
'William Lobb'
Moss
Laffay 1855

'Cardinal de Richelieu'
Gallica
Netherlands pre-1800

'Duchesse de Montebello'
Gallica
Laffay pre-1829

'Reine des Centfeuilles'
Centifolia
Belgium 1824

'Pink Grootendorst'
Perpetual shrub rose
Grootendorst 1923

'Alba Semiplena'
Alba

'Julia Mannering'
Sweet Brier
Penzance 1895

'Anja'
Perpetual shrub rose
Scholle 1976

'Belle Amour'
Alba

'Fürstin Pless'
('Princess Pless')
Perpetual shrub rose
Lambert 1911

'Pax'
Perpetual shrub rose
Pemberton 1918

Overleaf:
'Cristata'
Centifolia
Pre-1820

'Versicolor'
Gallica
Circa 1630

'Versicolor'
Gallica
Circa 1630

'Champion of the World'
Remontant hybrid
Woodhouse 1894

'Kathleen Harrop'
Bourbon
Dickson 1919

'Charles de Mills'
Gallica

'Petite de Hollande'
('Centifolia Minor')
Centifolia

'The Fairy'
Perpetual shrub rose
Bentall 1932

'Trigintipetala'
Damask

'Prosperity'
Perpetual shrub rose
Pemberton 1919

'Coralie'
Damask

'Golden Wings'
Perpetual shrub rose
Shepherd 1953

'City of York'
('Direktor Benschop')
Climbing rose
Tantau 1945

Overleaf:
Unnamed cultivated variety
Shrub rose
Tepelmann pre-1960

'Félicité Bohain'
Moss
United States of America
Pre-1866

'Charles Austin'
Shrub rose
Austin 1973

'Scarlet Fire'
('Scharlachglut')
Hip

'Scarlet Fire'
('Scharlachglut')
Shrub rose
Kordes 1952

'Lawrence Johnston'
Climbing rose
Pernet-Ducher 1923

Rosa multiflora
Wild rose
Japan

'Escapade'
Floribunda
Harkness 1967

'Madame Boll'
Portland
Boll 1845

'Elfriede'
Perpetual bush rose
Scholle 1985

'Madeleine Seltzer'
Climbing rose
Walter 1926

'Beauty of the Prairies'
Climbing rose
Feast 1843

'Officinalis'
Gallica
Pre-1300

'Autumn Delight'
Perpetual shrub rose
Bentall 1933

'Constance Spry'
Climbing rose
Austin 1961

'Ballerina'
Perpetual shrub rose
Bentall 1937

'Marguerite Hilling'
Perpetual shrub rose
Hilling 1959

Overleaf:
'Marytje Cazant'
Polyantha
Van Nes 1927

67

'Poulsen's Pearl'
Floribunda
Poulsen 1949

'Paulii'
Shrub rose
G. Paul pre-1903

71

'Elfenreigen'
Shrub rose
Krause 1939

'Black Boy'
Moss
Kordes 1958

'Danaë'
Perpetual shrub rose
Pemberton 1913

'Souvenir de la Malmaison'
Bourbon
Béluze 1843

'Königin von Dänemark'
('Queen of Denmark')
Alba
Booth 1816

'Madame Zöetmans'
Damask
Marest 1830

'Stanwell Perpetual'
Shrub rose
Lee and Kennedy 1838

'Johanna Röpcke'
Climbing rose
Tantau 1931

'Madame Hardy'
Damask
Hardy 1832

'Reine Victoria'
Bourbon
Schwartz 1872

Rosa × hibernica
Wild rose

'Lanei'
Moss
Laffay 1854

'Henri Martin'
Moss
Laffay 1863

'Lausitz'
Perpetual shrub rose
Berger 1959

Overleaf:
'Félicité Perpétue'
Sempervirens
Jacques 1827

84

'Celsiana'
Damask
Netherlands pre-1806

'Louise Odier'
Bourbon
Margottin 1851

'Climbing Cécile Brunner'
Climbing Polyantha
Hosp 1894

'Café'
Floribunda
Kordes 1953

'Triomphe de l'Exposition'
Remontant hybrid
Margottin 1855

'Gipsy Boy' ('Zigeunerknabe')
Shrub rose
Geschwind 1909

'Mozart'
Perpetual shrub rose
Lambert 1937

'Iceberg' ('Schneewittchen')
Perpetual shrub rose
Kordes 1958

'Gros Chou de Hollande'
Centifolia
Post-1820

'Gruss an Aachen'
Floribunda
Hinner 1909

'Fritz Nobis'
Shrub rose
Kordes 1941

'Duplex'
Shrub rose
Pre-1771

Overleaf:
'Salet'
Moss
Lacharme 1854

'Violacea'
Gallica
Pre-1806

'White Moss'
Moss
England 1788

'Maiden's Blush'
Alba
Pre-1629

Rosa corymbifera
Wild rose

'Muscosa'
Moss
Pre-1699

'Marytje Cazant'
Polyantha
Van Nes 1927

'Empereur du Maroc'
Remontant hybrid
Guinoisseau 1858

'Comtesse de Murinais'
Moss
Vibert 1843

'Paulii Rosea'
Shrub rose
Post-1903

'Weisse aus Sparrieshoop'
Perpetual shrub rose
Kordes 1962

Notes on the roses

Anny Jacob

Opposite:
'Adam Messerich'
Bourbon
Lambert 1920

'William Lobb'
Moss
Laffay 1855

PAGE 25. In England this
tremendously vigorous variety was sold
commercially under the name of
'William Lobb', while the French
preferred the title 'Duchesse d'Istrie'.
Planted by a garden fence, this rose's
long, thorny stems, with their rather
sparse foliage, can be given free rein. In
June they cover themselves with large,
semi-double, carmine-purple flowers,
whose petals are lighter on the reverse,
tending to lilac pink. The bristly moss
is green, and its resinous odour mingles
with the fragrance of the flowers. The
variously coloured blooms look
especially pretty in a vase.

'Cardinal de Richelieu'
Gallica
Netherlands pre-1800

PAGE 26. A rose unfolds. Its outer
matt-purple petals are already opened
wide, showing their pearl-white base.
The finely veined centre of the flower,
shimmering violet, is still completely
closed, promising us a densely petalled,
deep-purple, velvety rose, with a
perfume to match its charming colour.

This bushy shrub presents us with a
fine display of blooms every year in
June, if it is located in a semi-shaded
position and fed well. Grey-leaved
foliage forms a subdued backdrop in the
garden and in the vase.

The lineage and parentage of the
highly prized 'Cardinal de Richelieu'
are not known, for the old rose
catalogues seldom stated the breeder and
the plant's genealogy. Did the French
gardener Laffay give this name to one of
his own cultivated varieties around
1840, or did he simply rechristen the
much older Dutch 'Rose Van Sian'?

The English literature of the time
classified the variety as a 'Hybrid
China', and referred to it simply as
'Richelieu'. By 1870 the once so
numerous Gallica roses had almost
vanished from the catalogues, superseded
by the large-flowered remontant hybrids,
but many of these tough and hardy
varieties survive unrecognized in gardens
even today.

'Duchesse de Montebello'
Gallica
Laffay pre-1829

PAGE 27. The form of the delicate,
pale-pink flowers is quite perfect; they
look so fragile that they could be made
of porcelain. The scent of the bloom is
ethereal. The stems are very slender and
flexible, and the foliage is small and
grey green – both peculiarities of the
variety. The photograph shows a
thoroughly healthy plant; it has not
been underfed. 'Duchesse de
Montebello' always has a delicate look,
as if it needs support. Modern books
suggest that it embodies some qualities
of Alba and Centifolia, although early
rose books claim it to be a Chinensis
hybrid. In Italy it used to be grown tied
to pillars.

'Reine des Centfeuilles'
Centifolia
Belgium 1824

PAGE 28. A hundred-petalled rose was
mentioned in ancient times by the
writers Herodotus and Pliny, but they
were not speaking of a true Centifolia.
In the nineteenth century
Rosa × centifolia was thought to be
endemic to the Caucasus, but it is now
presumed to be a hybrid which was
raised in a garden, perhaps in Holland,
where it was first described around
1600. Who is not familiar with these
dense, nodding, globular roses from the
still lifes of the Dutch masters? But to
enjoy its authentic Centifolia fragrance,
you must find one in the garden. A
'Rosa centifolia' soap is a poor
substitute.

The name 'Reine des Centfeuilles' is
no exaggeration, for the flower has a
royal appearance among all its sisters.
Even the buds, with their pinnate calyx,
look attractive. The overhanging bush is
covered with large, densely filled, evenly
packed blooms of a beautifully pure
pink. Many people feel moved by the
flowers to compose their own still life in
a bowl, which then fills the whole
room with its scent.

'Pink Grootendorst'
Perpetual shrub rose
Grootendorst 1923

'Alba Semiplena'
Alba

'Julia Mannering'
Sweet Brier
Penzance 1895

'Anja'
Perpetual shrub rose
Scholle 1976

PAGE 29. *Rosa rugosa*, the rose with the wrinkled foliage, is outstandingly hardy, grows vigorously, and has densely spined stems. It is thought that the species can be recognized in old Chinese paintings produced around the year 1000, but it was only introduced into Europe from Japan in 1796.

It was not until the late nineteenth century that breeders began to exploit its qualities in cultivation, after many of the roses produced in France proved to be insufficiently hardy. The much praised white 'Blanc Double de Coubert' became commercially available in 1892, and originates from Cochet-Cochet, together with the purple 'Roseraie de l'Haÿ' with its luxuriant foliage. 'Conrad Ferdinand Meyer' was bred by the German amateur rose grower Dr H. Müller, and grows into a shrub the height of a man. It bears pink flowers as fine as any rose. All these cultivars have inherited the scent of *Rosa rugosa*.

'Pink Grootendorst', as the name suggests, comes from Holland. Its bizarre flowers are packed with curiously frayed petals, but the 'Carnation Rose' is almost scentless, and the petals do not fall but rather hang like mummies on the stiff-limbed bush with its scant covering of leaves.

PAGE 30. Until a few years ago all the rose books stated that the Greeks and Romans cultivated *Rosa × alba*. Today experts realize that the wild, single-flowered white rose mentioned by the ancient writers cannot be identified.

Like all other Alba roses 'Alba Semiplena' is outstandingly hardy, resistant to disease, and long-lived. In June the grey-green foliage of this tall shrub is overloaded with clusters of cream-coloured buds, which open to form softly scented, loosely packed, milk-white roses with shimmering stamens. Towards autumn the covering of brilliant-red hips is a wonderful sight.

PAGE 31. The simple beauty of this variety's flowers, similar to the dog rose, is captivating. The darker vein patterns of the light-pink petals run inward towards the white centre, where the bright green stigma can be seen in the middle of the ring of deep golden-coloured stamens. The light rose perfume mingles with the small, apple-scented leaves. The tough, vigorous, shrub rose 'Julia Mannering' is named after a woman who appears in Walter Scott's *Guy Mannering*. Its origins lie in remontant hybrids and *Rosa eglanteria*, the Scottish rambling rose, which is still known as *Rosa rubiginosa* on the Continent. In 1895 Lord Penzance made sixteen of his Sweet Brier hybrids available commercially. His white 'Flora McIvor', the carmine-red 'Lucy Ashton' and others are all named after characters in Scott's works. They are all large, bushy roses which flower only once.

PAGE 32. Offspring of the world-famous hybrid tea 'Duftwolke' ('Fragrant Cloud') and the shrub rose 'Maigold', 'Anja' has attractively slim buds, large, well-filled, bowl-shaped flowers, and light-yellow stamens. The petals fall off cleanly, and thus do not disfigure the clusters of blooms against the light-green foliage. At the end of May the shrub flowers abundantly, but the later blooms are produced more sparingly. 'Anja' has a reliable scent, but its colour varies. In cool weather it appears to be a simple, delicate pink, while on hot summer days it is paler, as if powdered with gold. The Westphalian amateur breeder succeeded in raising the children and the grandchildren of this hardy, medium-height shrub rose. From his collection of fine, unique cultivars, Ewald Scholle sold 'Sutton Place' to England, and I am personally indebted to him for 'Anja' – my beloved rose.

'Belle Amour'
Alba

'Fürstin Pless'
('Princess Pless')
Perpetual shrub rose
Lambert 1911

'Pax'
Perpetual shrub rose
Pemberton 1918

'Cristata'
Centifolia
Pre-1820

PAGE 33. In a monastery garden in Normandy Miss Nancy Lindsay discovered this unnamed foundling in 1950; she named it 'Belle Amour'. Ten years later Mr G. S. Thomas, the world's foremost expert on 'old roses', came across a very old bush of the same variety, growing against a cottage in Norfolk. In vain he studied old rose catalogues and rose books of the previous century, but there was nothing quite like it. Characteristic features of 'Belle Amour' are its aromatic fragrance, the suggestion of light salmon pink in its bowl-shaped, fairly densely petalled flowers, and the pronounced stamens. The photograph shows just how strong and thorny the stems of this powerful shrub are. It is thought that the forefathers of this beautiful foundling child are Damask, Alba and Ayrshire roses. 'Belle Amour' has conquered the hearts of rose growers everywhere, and the romantic name must have contributed to its success.

PAGE 34. Kaiser Wilhelm II and King Edward VII of England honoured 'the perfect, typical English beauty', with the golden hair and the forget-me-not blue eyes, who wore the world-famous Pless pearls to such incomparable effect. Daisy Cornwallis-West married young, and by 1891 felt like the tall rose standards in the giant park at Pless, planted out in formation, neatly supported, and seeming to bloom as if at command. She found herself yearning for a romantic rose garden.

She became familiar with the gardens of the Pless colliers, where 'Crimson Rambler' flowered just as abundantly as at Castle Fürstenstein. There her beloved new garden was laid out, exactly in the English style, and cared for by her Scottish gardener Todd. In 1907 the garden was inaugurated, and the nobility from many countries showed their admiration. In 1910 the 'fairy princess' graciously agreed to accept the dedication of a rose which fitted her own image. A hint of yellowish pink in the centre of the large, densely packed, white flowers, a subdued fragrance, a touch of green on the globular buds, a vigorous bush with light-coloured foliage: that is Peter Lambert's 'Fürstin Pless' – a perfect English beauty.

PAGE 35. When the Second World War ended and peace returned, the Americans gave the name 'Peace' to a rose bred by Francis Meilland; in Germany this variety is known as 'Gloria Dei'. In 1918 the popular yearning for peace was just as strong, and the Latin name 'Pax' was dedicated to one of the Rev. Joseph Pemberton's finest cultivated roses. Pemberton had become so fascinated by rose breeding that he had abandoned his spiritual calling in favour of raising roses.

'Pax' is a seedling of Peter Lambert's white shrub rose 'Trier', but its pointed, creamy yellow buds, from which the large petals unfold so elegantly, were probably inherited from its father, a hybrid tea. The very large, open, fairly loosely petalled roses contrast splendidly with the dark-green foliage, and how deliciously they are scented. It is hardly surprising that this vigorous variety with its superabundance of blooms, and its tendency to spread over walls, won the gold medal of the National Rose Society in 1919. This is the highest honour which a rose can attain in England.

PAGES 36/37. A variety which has always caught the imagination of man. The French called it 'Chapeau de Napoléon', because the tightly closed bud reminded them of Napoleon's hat. The English were content with 'Crested Moss', but it is not a Moss rose. In Germany the colloquial name is simply 'Hahnenkammrose' ('Cockscomb Rose'). Its strange appearance is due to the parsley-like outgrowths at the margins of the calyx. It could be a sport of a Centifolia, or perhaps an accidental seedling. In 1811 Guerrapain described a similar form, which he had obtained from Holland.

The Renaissance princes had their court dwarfs and other curiosities, and made collections of anything out of the ordinary. Gardeners have always had a weakness for the capricious offerings of nature, and the artist has licence to develop the highly unusual into the monstrous.

In the garden 'Cristata' is really a normal Centifolia, perhaps a little more erect in habit. The pure-pink, well-filled flowers are strongly scented. As the bizarre sepals are retained even when flowering is finished, they make splendid subjects for unusual flower arrangements.

'Versicolor'
Gallica
Circa 1630

'Versicolor'
Gallica
Circa 1630

'Champion of the World'
Remontant hybrid
Woodhouse 1894

'Kathleen Harrop'
Bourbon
Dickson 1919

PAGE 38. The large, loosely filled flowers of 'Versicolor' are a true delight; every individual bloom is unique, for the colour patterns are never the same. Crimson red and blush, irregularly splashed and striped, sometimes with delicate gradations of colour, now and again a petal with clearly separated colours. The large clusters of yellow stamens look like the dot on an 'i'; this is a fragrant masterpiece of nature. The foliage is strong, and the bush produces flowers in profusion.

PAGE 39. Every rose book since the first has related the appealing story of Fair Rosamund, the lover of Henry II, who died in 1177. This rose is said to have been dedicated to her memory. None of the story is true. Jack Harkness, the English rose grower and author, claims that this rose, also known as 'Rosa Mundi', had been found a few years earlier in Norfolk, growing on a branch of the ordinary red rose *Rosa gallica officinalis*. His source was *The Garden*, written by Sir Thomas Hammer in 1659. The English expert Bean refers to Rea's *Flora* of 1665 and states that 'Rosa Mundi' is described there. Nothing is known of its origins.

PAGE 40. Originally this rose was called 'Mary Woodhouse', probably after the wife of the American grower based in Vermont, but it was also sold commercially as 'Mrs De Graw'. The few varieties bred in America in the nineteenth century did not find immediate acceptance in Europe.

'Champion of the World' starts flowering early, but it is some time before the firm buds unfold their dense contents to form large, pure-pink roses, which exude a sweet scent. The erect shrub is disease-resistant, remontant and hardy.

PAGE 41. A soft, feminine sport of the famous, domineering and gaudy 'Zéphirine Drouhin'. The pointed buds are the colour of a young girl's unadorned lips; the light, airy flowers, mother-of-pearl pink and sweetly scented: set against the light-green foliage, the overall picture is captivating. Such beauty would melt the hardest heart! When the long summer holidays come, 'Kathleen Harrop' also enjoys a six-week rest. In September the slightly overhanging, medium-height bush produces its second flowers, which are not so abundant this time. They are a joy to behold and we look forward to the next year.

'Charles de Mills'
Gallica

PAGE 42. If this variety is really the same as 'Bizarre Triomphant', then it existed before 1811. An Englishman named Mills lived in Rome around 1840. He possessed a famous rose garden, described in Loiseleur-Deslongchamps' book *La Rose* of 1844. Perhaps this rose has its origins there. It is often extremely difficult to identify the old Gallica varieties; the more so since many of them are uncommonly similar.

The illustration shows a perfect bloom. All the petals finely folded and evenly arranged, the centre of the flower prominent, and the much prized hollow in evidence. It shows the dark shadows on the velvety, wine-red inner surface of the petals, as well as the slightly lighter-toned reverse. Imagine a light fragrance, and you have it. The almost spineless bush, with its dark foliage, grows upright.

'Petite de Hollande'
('Centifolia Minor')
Centifolia

PAGE 43. This is a genuine hundred-petalled rose, albeit with smaller blooms than 'Centifolia Major'. However, in its fragrance and profusion of flowers, the 'small Centifolia' is superior to its larger sister. Both plants develop into fine, overhanging shrubs.

'The Fairy'
Perpetual shrub rose
Bentall 1932

PAGE 44. 'The Fairy' was the name given to this low-growing rose by Bentall, Pemberton's successor. It is a sport of the climbing rose 'Lady Godiva', which casts a spell over our gardens from the beginning of July to Advent. Large clusters of small, rosette-like flowers of the finest pink, set off against small, deep-green, glossy foliage. It forms a neat, rounded shrub, as tall and wide as a table, and needs no protection. The more flowering stems are cut, the more strongly they come through again.

There was once a young lady who asked for 'The Fairy' for her wedding day. The loosely-knit garland looked very attractive in her blonde hair, and the light bouquet was easy for the bride to handle. The bridegroom was sceptical at first, but eventually he had a buttonhole made. Since that time many wedding guests have kept the versatile 'Fairy' in their gardens.

'Trigintipetala'
Damask

PAGE 45. Dr Dieck, who possessed a large arboretum at Zöschen near Magdeburg, brought 'Trigintipetala' back from the rose-growing region near Kazanluk in Bulgaria, and made it available commercially in 1889. At the time attempts were being made to cultivate roses for the extraction of oil in the Magdeburg, Steinfurth and Karlsruhe areas of Germany. The quality was evidently outstanding, but the yield small.

The loosely filled, pink flowers of 'Trigintipetala' appear in clusters, and its fragrance is exquisite. The relatively light-coloured foliage and the spiny stems are typical of Damask varieties. 'Trigintipetala' is more suitable as a source of perfumes than as a garden bush.

'Prosperity'
Perpetual shrub rose
Pemberton 1919

PAGE 46. Against the dark, glossy
foliage of this somewhat lax-growing
shrub, the large clusters of ivory-
coloured buds stand out well. The
interior of the opening bloom glows as
a delicate yellow, which fades steadily as
it develops into rosettes. The fragrance is
as soft and gentle as the colouring.
'Prosperity' continues flowering for a
considerable time.

'Coralie'
Damask

PAGE 47. Nobody knows the origins of
this rose, nor when it first appeared.
From its fat, globular buds it is clear
that the flowers will be densely packed
with petals. The medium-sized pure-
pink roses grow lighter toward the
centre, as the outer petals curl inward
and the stamens become visible in the
middle of the smaller, inner petals.
Small, grey-green foliage covers the
overhanging branches.

'Golden Wings'
Perpetual shrub rose
Shepherd 1953

PAGE 48. The American Roy E.
Shepherd dispensed with many old
wives' tales in his book *History of the
Rose* of 1954. His description of this
variety, which he raised himself, is
excellent: 'The large, single sulphur-
yellow blossoms have prominent amber
stamens and are produced abundantly
throughout the summer on a vigorous
4-foot plant . . .'

'City of York'
('Direktor Benschop')
Climbing rose
Tantau 1945

PAGE 49. This rose travelled abroad as
'City of York' and won the American
Rose Society's National Gold Medal
Certificate in 1950. The glossy, leathery
foliage on the long, powerful stems
forms a perfect backdrop for the creamy
white, medium-sized flowers, whose
loosely packed petals show off the
golden-yellow stamens beautifully. The
scented clusters of flowers are produced
in great profusion. This invariably
healthy variety was cultivated by
Mathias Tantau senior, and there are
some glorious old examples of it in the
rose garden at l'Haÿ.

Unnamed cultivated variety
Shrub rose
Tepelmann pre-1960

PAGES 50/51. An unnamed seedling
cultivated by a forgotten rose grower –
one little tile in a mosaic of a life which
was connected with roses from the
cradle to the grave. Hugo Tepelmann
was born in Ratzeburg, in the extreme
north of Germany, in 1880. His father,
a teacher who loved roses, was one of
the founder members of the German
Rose Society in 1883. In 1890 he
published the *Rose Name Interpreter*,
whose purpose was to 'lead gardeners
through the maze of foreign rose names'.
At that time there were very few roses
in existence which had been cultivated
in Germany.

His son Hugo was a mechanical
engineer. He studied Mendel's laws of
heredity, and cultivated roses. He
produced a genealogical index of rose
varieties, a work which kept him
occupied for decades. A small number
of his shrub rose varieties became
available commercially, among them
'Frau Geheimrat Spaeth' and 'Gela
Tepelmann', which he dedicated to his
wife, the daughter of Herr Gnau, the
'Rose Professor'. When he died, at the
age of 81, he was already forgotten. The
Sangerhausen rose garden took over
Hugo Tepelmann's unpublished works
and his unnamed seedlings.

'Félicité Bohain'
Moss
United States of America
Pre-1866

PAGE 52. With its dense covering of
moss on the flower stems, the sepals also
covered with greenish-brown moss, this
American cultivar is a genuine Moss
rose. Its moss has a resinous odour, its
pretty, medium-sized, pink flowers a
sweet scent. The small clusters of
flowers on the erect bush are a perfect
complement to a simple Biedermeier
vase.

'Charles Austin'
Shrub rose
Austin 1973

PAGE 53. This beautiful rose bears the
name of the father of its raiser. David
Austin is an Englishman who crosses
'old' roses with modern varieties, and
obtains shrub roses with the old-
fashioned form of flower, but often in
colours which are entirely new. Some of
these roses are remontant. 'Charles
Austin' develops into a pretty shrub
with light-green foliage, producing very
large, apricot-yellow roses, densely
petalled. Its scent is exquisite, its colour
tends to lighten with time. Its first
flowers are produced in abundance, and
further, though fewer, flowers are
produced later.

'Scarlet Fire'
('Scharlachglut')
Hip

PAGE 54. By late July 'Scarlet Fire' has
finished producing its large clusters of
flowers. From then until autumn the
very large, greenish-orange hips mature.
At the same time the very extended,
pinnate sepals dry out, producing
formations similar to a stag's antlers.
The extraordinarily beautiful hips are a
welcome decoration for garlands on All
Saints' Day, and even for Advent.

The unbelievable variety of sepal
forms is described in the very interesting
article 'Formvariationen der Kelchblätter
der Rose' ('Variations in the Form of
Rose Sepals') written by Dietrich
Woessner (the 'Father of Roses') in
Rosa Helvetica of 1987.

'Scarlet Fire'
('Scharlachglut')
Shrub rose
Kordes 1952

'Lawrence Johnston'
Climbing rose
Pernet-Ducher 1923

Rosa multiflora
Wild rose
Japan

'Escapade'
Floribunda
Harkness 1967

PAGE 55. Wilhelm Kordes liked to experiment with the descendants of wild roses and old roses. His aim was to improve the hardiness of shrub roses. The mother of 'Scarlet Fire' is 'Alika', a brilliant-red Gallica found in Russia around 1900, with large, scented flowers. The father is 'Poinsettia', a red rose grown for flower production under glass. The result of this union is a spreading shrub with dull-green foliage, which contrasts well with the young, reddish shoots. The name 'Scarlet Fire' ('Scharlachglut') is entirely appropriate. The very large, bowl-shaped flowers with the extended stamens are well-nigh luminous, and make a glorious sight.

PAGE 56. A sister seedling of the famous 'Rêve d'Or', which was made available commercially in 1923. Major Johnston obtained the unnamed seedling, and from then on a wall in the famous Hidcote garden has been a mass of golden-yellow flowers, at the beginning of the rose season. After 1948 the Sunningdale Nurseries produced the variety commercially under the name 'Lawrence Johnston'. It is a scented climbing rose which produces small quantities of flowers after the main crop.

PAGE 57. Like rays of light from tiny magic candles the stamens of this small, simple, wild rose stand out against the brilliant white petals. Each bloom is beautifully formed, but together they make giant clusters of flowers. If allowed to grow without constraint, the plant develops into a giant shrub which produces in the autumn masses of small, round, red hips. They are an ideal addition to autumn bouquets.

Densely petalled garden forms of *Rosa multiflora* were brought from Japan to Europe around 1800, while the simple *Rosa multiflora* was introduced into France in 1860.

PAGE 58. Jack Harkness, who began to breed roses in 1962, chose as his two parent varieties a pink hybrid tea which had gained many prizes, and 'Baby Faurax', a very low-growing, violet Polyantha of the 1920s. The result was 'Escapade', whose twelve-petalled, lilac-pink, shell-shaped flowers with the lighter centre have delighted many gardeners. The lightly scented flowers are produced in great clusters, which harmonize wonderfully well with the light-green, glossy foliage. 'Escapade' can be grown as a bush rose of moderate height, and the flower stems are well suited to display in a vase. Its raiser, Vice-President of the Royal National Rose Society, edited the widely appreciated Rose Annual. He has also written a whole series of outstanding books on roses. His book *The Makers of Heavenly Roses* is a highly amusing read, and yet crammed full of useful information. Many old wives' tales about roses are finally laid to rest in it.

'Madame Boll'
Portland
Boll 1845

'Elfriede'
Perpetual bush rose
Scholle 1985

'Madeleine Seltzer'
Climbing rose
Walter 1926

'Beauty of the Prairies'
Climbing rose
Feast 1843

PAGE 59. There is an appealing story, still in circulation, that *Rosa portlandica* was found by the Duchess of Portland close to the ancient city of Paestum, where once, according to Virgil, the twice-flowering rose of Paestum was grown. In fact, Virgil's text had been translated incorrectly, and the famous 'Duchess of Portland' has now been relegated to plain 'Portlandica'. Under this name it has been available commercially in England since 1775. 'Madame Boll' is the most prolific flowering of all Portland roses in cultivation today. Throughout the season the upright bush with its neat foliage is covered with large, closely filled, pink flowers, which are well scented. The famous Dean Hole praised its virtues as early as 1869. To the French it still rated as one of 'les plus belles' in 1912, when the Portland rose era was long since past.

The breeder of 'Madame Boll' was a Swiss gardener who had emigrated to New York. Daniel Boll's home was either in the canton of Bern, where in 1764 the lord of Graffenried had a rose collection numbering 46 varieties, or in Winterthur, like the rose painter Bertha Reinhart, whose entrancing pictures are only known from her rose book of 1892.

PAGE 60. 'Elfriede' was born in the Westphalian village of Seppenrade, in the garden of the amateur rose grower Ewald Scholle. A bush rose, which remains reasonably compact, it dresses its neat-leaved stems with clusters of buds at the very beginning of June. Slender roses, similar in form to the pure-bred species, spring from the buds, the yellowish undersides of their petals giving them almost a salmon-pink tint. How graceful are the large, broad, open roses, crowned with golden stamens! And how beautifully perfumed, the scent only dissipating when the petals fall. 'Elfriede' flowers indefatigably in the garden and makes a wonderful display indoors. A perpetual reminder of Elfriede Klose, who loved roses so dearly.

PAGE 61. Louis Walter was a senior postal official in the Alsatian town of Zabern, now known as Saverne. A rose society was founded there in 1898, and a rose garden was established soon after, which still exists today. Like its mother, the climbing rose 'Tausendschön', 'Madeleine Seltzer' has thornless stems, and flowers equally prolifically. In June its glossy foliage contrasts with massed clusters of globular, ivory-coloured buds, mixed in with open, bowl-shaped, well-filled roses. Its flowers are resistant to the weather, and the bush itself is hardy. Louis Walter produced about fifty cultivated varieties which are still known today. The most famous was his 'Yellow Moss', which he sold to America in 1931.

PAGE 62. *Rosa setigera*, the Prairie Rose, was named 'Rosier d'Amérique' by Michaux, and is endemic to the Midwest of the United States of America. It was first brought to Europe in 1810. Geschwind used it to breed his beautiful 'Erinnerung an Brod' ('Remembrance of Brod', 1886) and in the United States William Prince used it for the first experiments with rose cultivation, followed by the Feast brothers of Baltimore. 'Beauty of the Prairies', which was also known as 'Queen of the Prairies', was the first American rose to win a medal. It was the first of the Feast roses to become available commercially, and was probably a cross with a form of Gallica. The large, spherical buds are very pretty, as are the clusters of open, densely filled flowers, of a deep-pink hue, occasionally finely striped. A hardy, vigorous variety.

'Officinalis'
Gallica
Pre-1300

PAGE 63. The name of this species is a clear indicator of the original reason for which it was grown. It was used primarily for pharmaceutical purposes. Since the Middle Ages 'Officinalis' has been cultivated commercially around the French town of Provins, from which its alternative name is taken: 'Provins Rose'.

The fairly open, carmine-red flowers of 'Officinalis' have an exquisite fragrance, and in autumn the shrub has a colourful mass of red hips.

'Autumn Delight'
Perpetual shrub rose
Bentall 1933

PAGE 64. The pretty name is a reminder of the rich colours of autumn flowers. When the pointed buds peep out of the sepals, they show apricot colours, but the large, completely open, single roses are pure white, relieved only by the orange stamens. The clusters of flowers stand out well from the glossy foliage of this medium-height shrub.

'Constance Spry'
Climbing rose
Austin 1961

PAGE 65. The first cultivated variety produced by David Austin was a cross between the Gallica 'Isis' and the modern Floribunda 'Dainty Maid'. It is dedicated to the memory of a woman who not only loved old roses, but also had incomparable skills as a flower arranger and cookery writer.

Large bunches of long-stemmed flowers can be taken from this rose without any anxiety, for its branches tend to hang down. When the flowers are opening they are truly spherical, and they always open out well to form densely packed, bowl-shaped blooms. The large roses have a very characteristic aromatic scent. In autumn this tall climbing rose is decorated with large, orange-coloured hips. Though often described as a shrub, it is of very lax growth and best grown on a wall or fence.

'Ballerina'
Perpetual shrub rose
Bentall 1937

PAGE 66. Tiny buds, tinged with carmine, mixed in with exquisitely beautiful miniature dog roses with golden filaments and the older, fading blooms; the overall effect is of a large Phlox umbel. Like tiny ballerinas they nod and rock in the breeze, allowing a few tired petals to fall on to the small, glossy foliage on the elegantly overhanging branches. If the withered remains of the flowers are not removed, orange-red pearls of the hips follow.

'Marytje Cazant'
Polyantha
Van Nes 1927

'Poulsen's Pearl'
Floribunda
Poulsen 1949

'Paulii'
Shrub rose
G. Paul pre-1903

'Marguerite Hilling'
Perpetual shrub rose
Hilling 1959

PAGE 67. A sport of the cream-white 'Nevada', a Moyesii hybrid, raised by the Spaniard Pedro Dot. The broad, spineless shrub with its light-coloured foliage looks good throughout the season, but in mid-June it is covered with very large, almost single flowers of a deep-pink hue. The beauty of the single flower is more effective when the shrub begins to flower again early in August, at which time the pointed buds and the beautiful stamens are a wonderful sight.

PAGES 68/69. Innumerable sports of Polyantha roses were available commercially around 1930. At that time Dutch gardeners usually propagated very large numbers of a small range of sorts. The inevitable result was that many mutations occurred, some of them showing no more than slight colour variations compared with the stock varieties.

The delicately coloured 'Marytje Cazant' is a sport of the cherry-red 'Jessie', itself a sport of the brilliant-red 'Phyllis', which in turn is a seedling from the ruby-red 'Mme Norbert Levavasseur'. This is a seedling of the climbing rose 'Crimson Rambler', which was famous for its large clusters of flowers; this variety was introduced from Japan in 1893, where it had been cultivated for a long time.

PAGE 70. Of all the beautiful Floribunda roses cultivated in Denmark by the Poulsen family, 'Poulsen's Pearl' is the most noble. The basic colour of the flowers is pink, but they show a wide range of hue. The tight, pointed buds are a definite salmon pink, which appears to merge increasingly into the reddish anthers as the five wave-edged petals are rolled back. When the petals begin to fade and wither, the stamens turn inwards on themselves. Since 'Poulsen's Pearl' flowers abundantly and in clusters, this miracle of nature is one that we can all enjoy.

PAGE 71. The appearance of this variety indicates its lineage: it is thorny like a Rugosa and tends to creep along the ground like an Arvensis. The large, pure-white flowers with their yellow stamens appear in clusters. Its petals are twisted like the sails of a windmill. The foliage is dark and rough. 'Paulii' is often used as ground cover.

'Elfenreigen'
Shrub rose
Krause 1939

'Black Boy'
Moss
Kordes 1958

'Danaë'
Perpetual shrub rose
Pemberton 1913

'Souvenir de la Malmaison'
Bourbon
Béluze 1843

PAGE 72. In 1913 Wilhelm and Max Krause founded a tree nursery in Surrey. The two men spent the years from 1914 to 1917 in an internment camp on the Isle of Man, and during this period a friendship was established which proved to be lifelong. The twenty-two roses raised by Max Krause are a memorial to them.

In 1933 his famous black rose 'Nigrette' became available commercially, and in 1935 Wilhelm Kordes won the gold medal of the National Rose Society with his beautifully scented hybrid tea 'Crimson Glory'. He produced a pretty, pink seedling of the Macrantha hybrid 'Daisy Hill' which he named 'Raubritter'. 'Elfenreigen' was a further offspring of the same mother variety.

PAGE 73. A very interesting cross. The Floribunda 'Minna Kordes', whose father was the beautifully scented 'Crimson Glory', was crossed with the old Moss rose 'Nuits de Young' (also known as 'Black Moss'). The result was extremely successful, and 'Black Boy' is a wonderful sight. Very large, deep-red, exquisitely scented roses, their strong stems covered with bristly, reddish moss. The upright plant produces flowers in such abundance that stems can be cut almost at will.

PAGE 74. A golden rain fell on Danaë when Zeus made love to her. The English rose 'Danaë' presents us with golden hues from the bud right through to the fruit. In November, a bunch of 'Danaë' is a marvellous combination of the last buds, shimmering like red gold, the faded ivory-coloured blooms with golden yellow corolla, and clusters of orange-coloured hips, glowing against the plant's glossy foliage. The final scene in the rose drama.

PAGE 75. During the lifetime of Empress Josephine, the rose garden of La Malmaison was famous. It had been laid out by André Dupont, who was born in the Palatinate region of Germany. The roses needed to complete the collection were brought from every possible source, even from Schloss Wilhelmshöhe at Kassel, where Napoleon's brother Jerome resided after 1806. No register of the roses grown at Malmaison has ever been found. Josephine died in 1814, and Redouté's paintings are more a record of the roses popular at the time than of the roses in her garden.

The French rose grower Béluze, who produced a whole series of Bourbon roses, was quite evidently an admirer of Emperor Napoleon. In December 1840 Napoleon's ashes were buried in the Invalides, and in 1841 the rose 'Cendres de Napoléon' appeared. 'Souvenir du Petit Roi de Rome' and 'Impératrice Eugénie' followed. Thomas Rivers recorded in 1843 several light-coloured Bourbon roses cultivated by Béluze.

'Souvenir de la Malmaison' is probably the most famous Bourbon rose. Its delicate-pink colour and low habit make it suitable for a wide range of garden uses.

'Königin von Dänemark'
('Queen of Denmark')
Alba
Booth 1816

PAGE 76. This seedling from 'Maiden's Blush' was produced in James Booth's nursery in 1816. Booth was a Scot who lived in Flottbeck, near Hamburg, then under Danish rule. The rose became available commercially as 'Königin von Dänemark' in 1826 and is dedicated to Caroline Matilda, the consort of Christian VII; in other words it was a homage to the reigning sovereign.

The symmetrical pink roses of the 'Königin von Dänemark', its scent, its healthy grey-green foliage and its compact form make it ideal for many gardens.

'Madame Zöetmans'
Damask
Marest 1830

PAGE 77. The Damascene, or Damask, roses have always comprised a small group among the old roses. Characteristic features include loosely filled, nodding flowers and a fine fragrance. White and deep-pink colours predominate.

The scented, pinkish-white blooms of 'Madame Zöetmans' show a slightly stronger tint towards the centre, where a small green eye is visible. The bush is of medium height, and possesses a dense covering of light-coloured foliage.

'Stanwell Perpetual'
Shrub rose
Lee and Kennedy 1838

PAGE 78. The petals are so thin, and of such a delicate shade of pink, that they appear translucent, even though the flowers are very densely filled. The bush is very thorny, and the foliage small. Its first flowers are produced in abundance, but there are occasional subsequent blooms. The scented flowers look charming in a vase.

'Johanna Röpcke'
Climbing rose
Tantau 1931

PAGE 79. We have Mathias Tantau senior to thank for around 50 varieties, amongst them a few extremely beautiful ones, which have survived in the Sangerhausen rose garden. Around 1930 he experimented with the varieties 'Ophelia' and 'Dorothy Perkins'; 'Johanna Röpcke' is a child of the union. Year after year this plant, with its long, reddish, thornless stems, is densely covered with large clusters of scented pink flowers. The colour ranges from pink to yellowish. The light-green foliage is attractive, and always looks healthy.

'Madame Hardy'
Damask
Hardy 1832

'Reine Victoria'
Bourbon
Schwartz 1872

Rosa × hibernica
Wild rose

'Lanei'
Moss
Laffay 1854

PAGE 80. J. A. Hardy was a subject of Marie Antoinette, and died, a Freeman of the Third Republic, as Curator Emeritus of the Luxembourg Gardens. The rose collection of the Luxembourg Palace, later to become so famous, was based on the 218 varieties and species of rose which the Palatinate gardener André Dupont cultivated in Paris in 1813. The collection comprised 2000 varieties, most of them French. In the garden foreign imports were allowed to acclimatize, and the qualities of newly cultivated roses were checked. The highly prolific white *Rosa clinophylla*, a native of India and China, was also grown there. This species is said to be the ancestor of two famous roses: the Persica hybrid × *Hulthemosa hardii* and 'Madame Hardy', which lately has been classified as a 'Damask Centifolia'. All its large, extremely densely petalled, bowl-shaped blooms are scented, and soon turn entirely white. However, not all of them have the highly prized small, light-green 'something' in the centre, which the American Roy Shepherd so unromantically termed 'a malformed bud'. Seventy roses cultivated by J. A. Hardy are known, but the rose which he dedicated to his wife is loved by more people today than ever before.

PAGE 81. This characteristic Bourbon rose was cultivated by the Schwartz rose-growing family in Lyon. It is one of the six varieties which were dedicated to Queen Victoria. The globular buds are a strong pink in colour, while the hemispherical flowers with their shell-shaped petals are closer to the pink of old roses. The lightly scented flowers look quite portly compared with the pointed, light-green foliage of this upright bush.

PAGE 82. The 'Irish rose' was discovered near Belfast by a Mr Templeton in 1802. This natural hybrid, a cross between *Rosa canina* and *Rosa spinosissima*, was enthusiastically received by Marie Henriette von Chotek – the 'Rose Duchess'. She praised its hardiness and elegant form, and was delighted by the single flowers with their dog-rose scent, and the grey-green foliage.

PAGE 83. This Moss rose is dedicated to the English gardener Lane. It is one of the 388 varieties cultivated by Jean Laffay, who began growing roses around 1820, when he was head gardener at Ternaux. There is hardly any class of rose to which he has not contributed new varieties. Around 1845 he concentrated on remontant Moss roses and had high hopes for his efforts, but even 'Lanei' does not produce many flowers after the first flush. In June the thorny, moss-covered buds are a delight, followed by the carmine lilac of the large, scented, well-filled flowers, which often have a pretty tinge of blue. The upright shrub is very neat in appearance.

'Henri Martin'
Moss
Laffay 1863

PAGE 84. The powerful carmine red of
the large, moderately filled flowers glows
from afar in the garden, enticing the
onlooker to observe more closely the
robust bush with the prominent,
greenish, thorny moss. It is always a
good idea to collect some of the long
flower stems and arrange them in the
house. They open well and have a
slightly aromatic scent, which seems
very appropriate to this rose, with its
masculine appearance.

'Lausitz'
Perpetual shrub rose
Berger 1959

PAGE 85. This rose originated in
Langensalza, a small town in the area
of Erfurt. In the 1930s the village of
Ufhoven, today incorporated into
Langensalza, was known as the 'first
rose village'.

Wilhelm Kordes's shrub roses
'Rosendorf Ufhoven' and
'Rosenwunder' were a form of greeting
to Langensalza, where the Berger family
began breeding roses in 1943. Walter
Berger produced the tall shrub rose
'Lausitz', whose healthy, light-green
foliage sets off so well the large clusters
of delicate-pink flowers with their
beautiful fragrance. The Berger family's
work was continued after 1960 by the
garden co-operative 'Roter Oktober'.
Frau Anni Berger was acclaimed as
'honorary people's rose breeder'. She is
the only woman in Germany who has
ever had success in raising new rose
varieties. Her brilliant-red climbing rose
'Rosenfest', with its massed clusters of
single roses, is an absolute delight.

'Félicité Perpétue'
Sempervirens
Jacques 1827

PAGES 86/87. The court gardener of
the Duke of Orléans enjoyed raising
roses based on *Rosa sempervirens*. This is
one of his most famous varieties.

Large clusters of buds cover the
glossy foliage only in June, after which
the opening, red-tinged buds mix in
with rosettes of densely packed, cream-
white flowers. The slightly aromatic
scent is shared by the low-growing, and
hence versatile, sport 'Little White Pet'.

'Celsiana'
Damask
Netherlands pre-1806

PAGE 88. This beautiful shrub rose
originated in Haarlem, and was also
sold commercially under the names
'Porcelaine' and 'La Triomphante'.
These names seem highly appropriate
to the variety. Its buds are comparable in
colour to the unembellished lips of a
young girl. Its large, loose, pink flowers
look as if they are made of silk. They
fade quickly in the sun, but the result is
only that the stamens glow all the more
strongly. The flower's sweet scent
matches its youthful appearance. It
develops into a well-formed bush with
grey-green foliage. In 1806 Thory
dedicated this variety to Monsieur Cels,
whose tree nursery in Paris had the
reputation of being the finest in Europe.

'Louise Odier'
Bourbon
Margottin 1851

PAGE 89. A thoroughly reliable
variety. The bush is of upright habit,
and its matt, light-coloured foliage is
permanently healthy. The large,
rounded roses are beautifully formed;
they are densely filled, and of a pure
pink which hardly varies. 'Louise
Odier' flowers reliably and prolifically
and over a long period. Its gentle scent
is always perceptible.

'Climbing Cécile Brunner'
Climbing Polyantha
Hosp 1894

PAGE 90. Climbing forms are
mutations – sports – of a low-growing
rose variety. 'Cécile Brunner', the
original form, is a cross between a
Polyantha and a genuine tea rose. This
is the reason for the slightly
overhanging, pointed buds, which
unfold so prettily, the tea-rose colour
and the characteristic scent. The plant
and foliage are graceful, as is every
aspect of the variety.

The widow of the Lyons rose
breeder Ducher dedicated this low-
growing rose to the daughter of the rose
grower Ulrich Brunner, who lived in
Lausanne. In the United States of
America the variety was known as 'The
Sweetheart Rose', and that is where
Hosp found this climbing sport, which
can attain a height of 13 feet.

'Café'
Floribunda
Kordes 1953

PAGE 91. Considering the era in
which it was produced, 'Café' possesses
a highly unusual colour: similar to
milky coffee with a slightly amber or
pinkish shimmer. The colour tends to
be more or less intense depending on
the weather, and it lasts longer in half-
shaded conditions. The large, olive-
green foliage forms a restrained
background to the neat, lightly scented
flower clusters of this knee-high,
prolifically flowering bush.

'Triomphe de l'Exposition'
Remontant hybrid
Margottin 1855

PAGE 92. This plant is one of the very
hardy, robust, free-flowering hybrids
which bloom for a second time in
autumn. The English named this class
'hybrid perpetual', although the plants
by no means flower continuously.

As is typical for roses cultivated in
this period, the large flowers are densely
packed with carmine-red petals, whose
surface looks as if it is covered with
velvet. The flowers have a fruity scent.

'Gipsy Boy'
('Zigeunerknabe')
Shrub rose
Geschwind 1909

PAGE 93. Raised by the forestry commissioner Rudolf Geschwind, this rose was made available commercially by Peter Lambert in 1909. Lambert gave a description of it in the rose magazine of the same year. As it is a seedling of the old 'Russeliana', it is unlikely that it can be categorized as a Bourbon rose, as is still claimed in many quarters.

In 1864 Geschwind published the first German rose book which described rose breeding in detail. His aim was to produce really hardy bush and climbing roses, which would not wither back to the ground when exposed to frost. He was the first German amateur rose breeder to achieve recognition in France and the United States of America.

'Gipsy Boy' is a vigorous, thorny shrub, whose well-filled, deep carmine-red flowers tend toward the violet. In the centre the golden stamens provide a rich glow. The clusters of flowers in the early summer make way for an attractive covering of hips in the autumn.

'Mozart'
Perpetual shrub rose
Lambert 1937

PAGE 94. 'Mozart' is one of the last roses produced by Peter Lambert, completing the cycle of cultivated shrub roses which began with the perpetual 'Trier' of 1904. In Germany his varieties were known as 'Lambertiana' roses. The Englishman Pemberton also chose 'Trier' as his starting point, and some of his shrub roses are still known as Musk hybrids today. Pemberton's 'Robin Hood' first became available in 1927, after his death, and Peter Lambert selected it as mother rose for 'Mozart', because of its prolific flush of single flowers. This moderately sized bush is ideal for the modern town garden. The small, single, brilliant-pink flowers, with their attractive white centres, are crammed together like a large umbel of Phlox. The rounded bush continues flowering until the late autumn. The bead-like hips are also very pretty.

'Iceberg'
('Schneewittchen')
Perpetual shrub rose
Kordes 1958

PAGE 95. This was the first of Reimer Kordes's varieties to win a gold medal from the Royal National Rose Society. It is also known as 'Fée des Neiges' and 'Schneewittchen' outside Britain, and is, unfortunately, sometimes planted as a bedding rose like a Floribunda. From the shrub rose 'Robin Hood' it has inherited its vigorous growth and rich mass of flowers, from the prize-winning white hybrid tea 'Virgo' its slender flowers, which are still good-looking even when completely open. The bush, with its glossy, dark-green foliage, continually provides new shoots, and it is possible to cut bouquets of flowers even on All Saints' Day.

'Gros Chou de Hollande'
Centifolia
Post-1820

PAGE 96. The Belgian author Gisèle de la Roche spent much of her life writing her commentary on Redouté's *Les Roses*, and she included this variety among the ancestors of Laffay's remontant hybrids. It is easy to believe that this broad-growing shrub has its origins in Centifolia and Bourbon roses. The buds are fat and tightly packed, the scent of the large, pure-pink flowers heavy.

'Gruss an Aachen'
Floribunda
Hinner 1909

PAGE 97. Although the Floribunda class was not established until after the Second World War, this variety, produced in 1909 by Wilhelm Hinner, still fits this category, now also known as 'Cluster-flowered bush'. Its mother is the very vigorous remontant hybrid 'Snow Queen'; its father a scented hybrid tea. 'Gruss an Aachen' is the ideal complement to old roses. The flat flowers are large, completely filled, and pinkish white in colour, tending to delicate salmon pink toward the centre. The low bush grows evenly, and remains in flower until the autumn.

'Gruss an Aachen' is an excellent bedding plant. The pure-white and pink sports are equally free-flowering. The climbing sport of 'Gruss an Aachen' is a jewel, and is seen far too rarely.

'Fritz Nobis'
Shrub rose
Kordes 1941

PAGE 98. Fritz Nobis was head of the Hamburg park known as 'Planten un Blomen'. Before the Second World War the gardens were planted with a mixture of harmonically arranged shrub roses, grasses and perennial plants. Nobis was a friend of Wilhelm Kordes, who dedicated to him one of his most beautiful shrub roses. The large, broad bush, whose thorny stems are densely covered with beautiful foliage, is an outstanding sight in June with its mass of roses. Its soft-pink tones and its shape of flowers are reminiscent of its great-grandmother 'Ophelia'. In autumn the orange-coloured hips make a fine show.

'Duplex'
Shrub rose
Pre-1771

PAGE 99. 'Duplex' belongs to the species *Rosa villosa*, which used to be called *Rosa pomifera*, and reminds us of something which Peter Lambert wrote in an old catalogue:

'The wild rose also has its beauty. Let us give it the chance to show what it can do.' This thought dates from a period in which few people had any time for wild roses.

This sort has been a resident of Schloss Wilhelmshöhe park since before 1771. Note the pure-pink, semi-open flowers of 'Duplex', its hairy buds and its grey-green foliage.

'Salet'
Moss
Lacharme 1854

PAGES 100/101. Who could deny himself the pure-pink flowers of the Moss rose from June to the first frosts? The old Moss rose 'Salet' has light-green foliage, and needs no more space than the modern 'Iceberg'; it will survive any winter. All the medium-sized, sometimes quartered flowers, are lightly scented.

'Violacea'
Gallica
Pre-1806

'White Moss'
Moss
England 1788

'Maiden's Blush'
Alba
Pre-1629

Rosa corymbifera
Wild rose

PAGE 102. The almost thornless, new branches of 'Violacea' are inclined steeply upward, and its small, dense foliage is beautifully rounded. The buds have strikingly long sepals, while the ten-petalled flowers are a velvety carmine red, lightening towards the centre. Yet what would the flowers be without the ring of golden stamens, which are left standing when the flower petals fall? In autumn the dark-red, globular hips appear on long stems.

PAGE 103. At some time before 1700 a pink-flowering *Rosa × centifolia* decided to cover its calyx and stems with thick moss. We know that this mutation appeared in the famous garden of the Leipzig senator Caspar Bose, as it is mentioned in *Hortus Bosianus*, written by Elias Peine in 1699. The Common Moss rose, 'Muscosa', was exported to England from the botanical gardens of Leyden. In 1788 and 1818 white sports were discovered in England, which were then christened 'White Moss'.

The fragrant flowers are white, with an extremely delicate pinkish tint. Sometimes this rose throws out a stem with pink flowers, reverting to the Common Moss rose, which apparently was first seen in Leipzig.

PAGE 104. 'The maidenly blushing rose, a variety of the White Rose'; thus wrote the lawyer Dr Rössig in the first German rose book, written in 1799, which was not intended for botanists. If we are to believe the English expert Bean, the flesh-coloured *Rosa incarnata* was described by Parkinson in 1629, but it was not until 1752 that Philip Miller gave it the popular name of 'Maiden's Blush'. In France it is known as 'Cuisse de Nymphe'.

Spherical buds, opening to form delicate-pink, densely petalled roses: this is the incomparably beautiful covering of the rounded shrub at the end of June.

PAGE 105. *Rosa corymbifera* is a close relative of the indigenous *Rosa canina* — the dog rose. How innocent and charming these snow-white hedge rose flowers are!

'Muscosa'
Moss
Pre-1699

'Marytje Cazant'
Polyantha
Van Nes 1927

'Empereur du Maroc'
Remontant hybrid
Guinoisseau 1858

'Comtesse de Murinais'
Moss
Vibert 1843

PAGE 106. Dense, soft moss covers the flower stems and buds of 'Muscosa', the Common Moss. Even its long sepals are covered with fern-like growths. The colour and form of the flower, and the habit of the bush, are very similar to *Rosa × centifolia*, of which it is a mutation. The first mention of a Moss rose is found in *Hortus Bosianus*, written by Elias Peine. He had observed 'Muscosa' in the garden of senator Caspar Bose at Leipzig before 1699.

PAGE 107. *Roses of Yesterday and Today* was the name of the catalogue which the American Dorothy Stemler published for many years. It was always an Aladdin's cave for rare varieties. Among them was the pink-flowering 'Marytje Cazant', a sport of the cherry-red 'Jessie' of 1909. The delights of 'Marytje Cazant' include the rounded buds which appear in great profusion, and which vary in hue from delicate salmon pink to almost white. This old Polyantha offers no scent, but its low, small-leaved bushes soon resume flowering, and their gentle colours make an ideal framework in which to plant old roses.

PAGE 108. An imposing name, appropriate for these large flowers. 'Empereur du Maroc' has deep-crimson petals with darker shading, the petals overlapping like roof tiles.

The scented flowers of this relatively low-growing remontant hybrid become shaded with violet when flowering is nearly over.

PAGE 109. Hard and bristly is the moss of 'Comtesse de Murinais', betraying its Damask lineage. The upright bush with its ribbed foliage is one of the first Moss roses to flower. The lovely buds are a clear pink, but the large, open, flat flowers fade to almost white. The fragrance of the small flower clusters is more resinous than sweet.

'Paulii Rosea'
Shrub rose
Post-1903

'Weisse aus Sparrieshoop'
Perpetual shrub rose
Kordes 1962

'Adam Messerich'
Bourbon
Lambert 1920

PAGE 110. 'Paulii Rosea' is a sport of the white 'Paulii', but is by no means such a vigorous grower as the latter. 'Paulii Rosea' produces pure, fine, pink flowers which lighten toward the centre, from where a cluster of stamens radiates.

At the end of June 'Paulii Rosea' is an entrancing sight, with a mass of rich, scented blooms, but later flowers are rare.

PAGE 111. A white sport of the pink-flowering shrub rose 'Sparrieshoop', with the same good qualities. A vigorous bush, covered with large, glossy, dark-green foliage, bearing upright flower stems. The wavy petal margins give the large, single flowers a carefree look, emphasizing the mass of stamens. This is a free-flowering variety which produces scented roses until late in the autumn. Both the 'Weisse aus Sparrieshoop' and its pink sister look good with old roses, for their beauty is timeless, and not subject to the whims of fashion.

These varieties bear the name of their birthplace, a small village in Schleswig-Holstein, which became world-famous for roses bred by the Kordes family.

PAGE 112. A product of Peter Lambert's work, this is a descendant of the fine Bourbon rose 'Louise Odier'. The new variety was tested in the garden of his enthusiastic rose-growing friend Adam Messerich, in the harsh climate of the Eifel, before it was made available commercially.

Every year the vigorous 'Adam Messerich' is the first Bourbon rose to flower. The light-green foliage is then covered with glowing, light-pink flowers, initially beaker-shaped. The blooms are quite loosely packed, which allows them to open in any weather. Large bunches of long-stemmed, scented roses can be cut from each shrub without ill effects, as the rather lax shrub always pushes out new shoots.

Sources

de l'Aigle, Alma, *Begegnung mit Rosen* (Hamburg 1957)

Bean, William Jackson, *Trees and Shrubs hardy in the British Isles* (Vol. 4: Ri-Z, 8th edition, revised 1980)

Coats, Peter, *Roses* (London 1962)

Die Rosensammlung zu Wilhelmshöhe (Kassel 1987, 3rd revised and enlarged edition)

Gravereaux, J., *La Malmaison: Les Roses de l'Impératrice Joséphine* (Paris 1912)

Harkness, Jack, *Roses* (London 1978)

Jäger, August, *Rosenlexikon* (Leipzig 1960)

Krüssmann, Gerd, *Rosen, Rosen, Rosen* (Berlin and Hamburg 1974)

Lejeune, Servais, *Der Rose Pilgerfahrt* (Hamburg 1983)

Redouté, P. J. and Thory, C. A. *Les Roses* (5th edition, Vol. 4 *Commentaire sur les roses de P. J. Redouté* by Gisèle de la Roche, Antwerp 1978)

Rosenverzeichnis Rosarium Sangerhausen (Sangerhausen 1976, 3rd edition)

Shepherd, Roy E., *History of the Rose* (reprinted New York 1978)

Schnack, Friedrich, *Rose – Königin der Gärten* (Munich 1961)

Stock, K. L., *Rose Books: A Bibliography of Books 1550–1975* (Milton Keynes 1984)

Testu, Charlotte, *Les Roses anciennes* (Paris 1984)

Thomas, G. S., *The Old Shrub Roses* (London 1983, revised edition)

Young, Norman, *The Complete Rosarian* (London 1971)